Puppies and Kittens & Pets, Oh My!

CUTE & EASY — CAKE TOPPERS

Cute & Easy Cake Toppers
Puppies, Kittens, Bunnies, Pets and more!

Contributors

Amanda Mumbray

Following a career in finance, Amanda Mumbray launched her cake business in 2010 and has gone from strength to strength, delighting customers with her unique bespoke creations and winning several Gold medals at various International Cake Shows. Amanda's **Clever Little Cupcake** company is based near Manchester, UK:
www.cleverlittlecupcake.co.uk

Elina Prawito

Elina Prawito is a cake designer based in Auckland, New Zealand. Her passion for cake design started when she made her son's 1st birthday cake in 2007 and fell in love with sugar art and cake design. 3 years later **bake-a-boo cakes** was born! You can view more of Elina's stunning work at:
www.bakeaboo.com

Helen Penman

Helen Penman has been designing cakes for over 15 years and her work has been featured in a wide range of cake books and magazines. She has also written several cake decorating and modelling books of her own, and runs a successful cake company from her home in Kent, UK.
www.toonicetoslice.co.uk

Lesley Grainger

Lesley Grainger has been imaginative since birth and has baked since she was old enough to hold a spatula. When life-saving surgery prompted a radical rethink, Lesley left a successful corporate career to pursue her passion for cake making. Lesley is based in Greenock, Scotland. Say 'hello' at:
www.lesleybakescakes.co.uk

First published in 2014 by Kyle Craig Publishing

Text and illustration copyright © 2014 Kyle Craig Publishing

Editor: Alison McNicol

Design: Julie Anson

ISBN: 978-1-908-707-44-4

A CIP record for this book is available from the British Library.

A Kyle Craig Publication

www.kyle-craig.com

Contents

8 Puppy Present!

12 Puppy Cupcakes

8 Lazy Dogs

18 In The Dog House

20 Turtles & Tortoises

22 Birthday Mice

24 Cheeky Bunny

26 Burrowing Bunnies

28 Cute Cats

32 Frog Prince

34 Hamster & Guinea Pig

36 Lazy Lizard

38 Kitten Cupcake Toppers

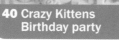

40 Crazy Kittens Birthday party

44 Wool and Kittens Cupcakes

Welcome!

Welcome to **'Puppies and Kittens and Pets, Oh My!'**, the latest title in the **Cute & Easy Cake Toppers Collection**.

Each book in the series focuses on a specific theme, and here we have compiled a gorgeous selection of beautiful cake toppers that will delight any kitten crazy, puppy-loving, pet fanatic or animal lover!

Whether you're an absolute beginner or an accomplished cake decorator, these projects are suitable for all skill levels, and we're sure that you will have as much fun making them as we did!

Enjoy!

Fondant/Sugarpaste/Gumpaste

Fondant/Sugarpaste – Ready-made fondant, also called ready to roll icing, is widely available in a selection of fantastic colours. Most regular cake decorators find it cheaper to buy a larger quantity in white and mix their own colours using colouring pastes or gels. Fondant is used to cover entire cakes, and as a base to make modelling paste for modelling and figures (see below).

Modelling Paste – Used throughout this book. Firm but pliable and dries faster and harder than fondant/sugarpaste. When making models, fondant can be too soft so we add CMC/Tylose powder to thicken it.

Gumpaste – Also known as 'Florist Paste'. More pliable than fondant, but dries very quickly and becomes quite hard, so it is widely used for items like flowers that are delicate but need to hold their shape when dry. Gumpaste can be made by adding Gum-Tex/Gum Tragacanth to regular fondant.

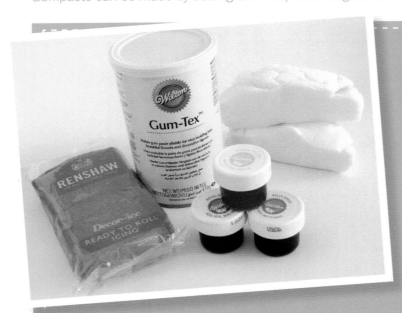

How to Make Modelling Paste

Throughout this book we refer to 'paste', meaning modelling paste. You can convert regular shop-bought fondant into modelling paste by adding CMC/Tylose powder, which is a thickening agent.

Add approx 1 tsp of CMC/Tylose powder to 225g (8oz) of fondant/sugarpaste. Knead well and leave in an airtight freezer bag for a couple of hours.

Add too much and it will crack. If this happens, add in a little shortening (white vegetable fat) to make it pliable again.

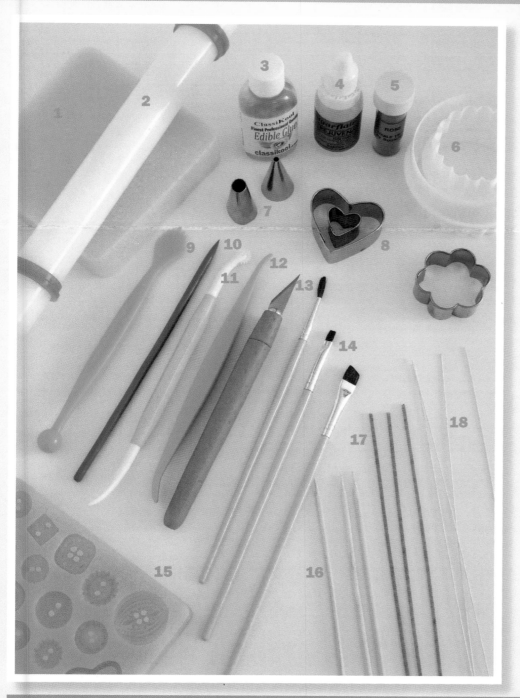

1 Foam Pad – holds pieces in place while drying.

2 Rolling pin – acrylic works better than wooden when working with fondant/paste.

3 Edible glue – essential when creating models. See below.

4 Rejuvenator spirit – mix with food colourings to create an edible paint.

5 Petal Dust, pink – for adding a 'blush' effect to cheeks.

6 Round and scalloped cutters – a modelling essential.

7 Piping nozzles – used to shape mouths and indents.

8 Shaped cutters – various uses.

9 Ball tool/serrated tool – another modelling essential.

10 Small pointed tool – used to create details like nostrils and holes.

11 Quilting tool – creates a stitched effect.

12 Veining tool – for adding details to flowers and models.

13 Craft knife/scalpel – everyday essential.

14 Brushes – to add finer details to faces.

15 Moulds – create detailed paste buttons, fairy wings and lots more.

16 Wooden skewers – to support larger models.

17 Spaghetti strands – also used for support.

18 Coated craft wire – often used in flower making.

Edible Glue

Whenever we refer to 'glue' in this book, we of course mean 'edible glue'. You can buy bottles of edible glue, which is strong and great for holding larger models together. You can also use a light brushing of water, some royal icing, or make your own edible glue by dissolving ¼ teaspoon tylose powder in 2 tablespoons warm water. Leave until dissolved and stir until smooth. This will keep for up to a week in the refrigerator.

Making Faces

The animal faces featured in this book vary in terms of detail and difficulty. If you're a complete beginner, you may opt to use simple shapes and edible pens to draw on simple features. As your confidence grows, you can use fondant for eyes and pupils, edible paint for features, or combine these methods for some great detailing.

 A veining tool will create indents for features.

 A mixture of fondant and black sugar pearls can create eyes, nose and eyebrows.

 Contrasting paste creates a cute muzzle.

 Pink petal dust adds blush to cheeks.

 Edible pens can be used to draw on simple features.

 Black fondant with white fondant or non-pareils make detailed eyes.

 When adding tiny pieces of fondant for eyes, use a moist fine brush.

When making small figures for cupcakes, it's great to place each on a topper disc, and place this on top of a lovely swirl of buttercream. This way the figure can be removed and kept, and the child can tuck into the main cupcake.

Regular round cutters are essentials, and there are also a great selection of embossing tools and sheets out there that, when pressed into your rolled paste, will create cool quilting effects on your disc. Make your discs first and allow them to harden before you fix your figures to them.

You can also combine a scalloped cutter with the point of a small, round piping nozzle to create discs with cut-out holes.

Plunger cutters are a great way to add cute details to your models. They cut and then 'push' each small piece out, making it easy to cut small flowers, leaves and shapes.

Painting Details

Many of the projects in this book have beautiful details painted onto the mini items. Mixing regular gel or paste food colouring, or lustre dusts, with rejuvenator spirit will create edible paint in any colour you need. Keep a small collection of fine paintbrushes handy too!

Coloured details – mix your regular food colouring with rejuvenator spirit to create edible paint.

White paint – Americolor Bright White gel paste colour is strong enough to paint on clear white details.

1 For the body of the box I have used a styrofoam sheet, but if you want it to be edible you can also use rice krispie treats, or cake covered with buttercream.

2 Thinly roll white paste and cut it the same size as your box.

3 Attach it to the top part of the box only.

4 Make another 4 squares of paste, the same width but the height needs to be slightly taller than the box. Allow to dry.

5 Once they are dry and set, glue them to the box.

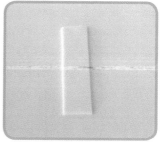

6 For the box ribbon, cut 4 white long rectangles, the same height as each side.

7 Attach them to the centre of the box on all four sides.

8 For the bow, make a long strip of white paste, approx. twice the length of the box, then cut the ends to make a pointed shape.

9 Gently make a soft pleat in the centre.

10 Flatten the middle part with your finger. Thinly brush the center with edible glue.

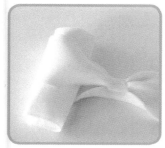

11 Place a roll of tissue and gently fold one side of the bow around the tissue and attach the pointy end to the center of the bow. Repeat on other side.

12 Carefully turn the bow around. Cut a rectangle shape for the middle of the bow.

13 Brush a little edible glue on the back then wrap it around the bow. Leave the tissue still in the bow until completely dry.

14 Now it is ready to be arranged on the cake.

15 To make the grey puppy, start by rolling some paste into a ball shape.

16 Then gently shape it into a cone shape. This will be the body.

17 Attach the body into the box and insert a support stick.

18 To make the puppy's collar, roll and cut a small round shape. Attach this to the top of the body.

19 For the paws, roll some paste into a long cone shape then make 3 cuts to shape the paw. Glue paws to the body and allow all to dry.

20 To make the head, roll out paste into a big round shape.

21 Attach this to the body and let it dry.

22 For the nose, roll out white paste and cut into a round shape.

23 Glue it to the bottom part of the head. Mark the fur lines and mouth using veining tool.

24 For the eyes, use two 4mm black sugar pearls. For eyebrows, shape 2 sausage shapes, slightly curved. For the nose, roll a small black oval.

25 Attach them to the face and make some fur lines on the eyebrows using veining tool.

26 For the ears, roll a cone shape then gently flatten the top. Slightly bend the ears and attach to the head.

27 Use a daisy plunger cutter for the blossom flower.

28 If you have one, shape the blossom flower paste using a blossom flower silicone mould and glue a white sugar pearl in the middle.

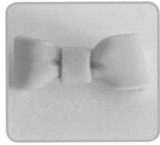

29 Make a mini bow using the same method as the bow for the present on the previous page.

30 Attach the bow and flower on the puppy. Finish off by dusting the cheeks and mouth with pink petal dust.

31 To make the white puppy, start by rolling white paste into a ball shape.

32 Then shape it into a cone shape. Insert support stick.

33 To make the collar, roll out light blue paste fairly thick and cut it into a round shape.

34 Attach this to the body.

35 For the legs, roll out some paste into a sausage shape, slightly flatten the top end.

36 Attach them to the body. Let this dry.

37 For the head, roll out a big egg shape of paste.

38 Attach it to the body.

39 Prepare the eyes, you will need two 4mm black sugar pearls. For the nose, roll out black paste into an oval shape.

40 Attach them to the face.

41 For the ears, roll a cone shape then gently flatten the top. Slightly bend the ears and attach to the head.

42 Finish it off by dusting the cheek and mouth with pink petal dust.

43 To make the gift box tissue, thinly roll white paste and cut it into a square shape.

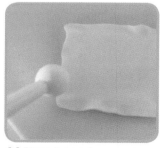

44 Place it on a foam pad and slightly thin out the edges using the ball tool.

45 Create soft pleats by making a small gathering in the centre of the square.

46 Make a few of these and arrange them in the box around the puppies to fill any gaps.

Puppy Cupcakes

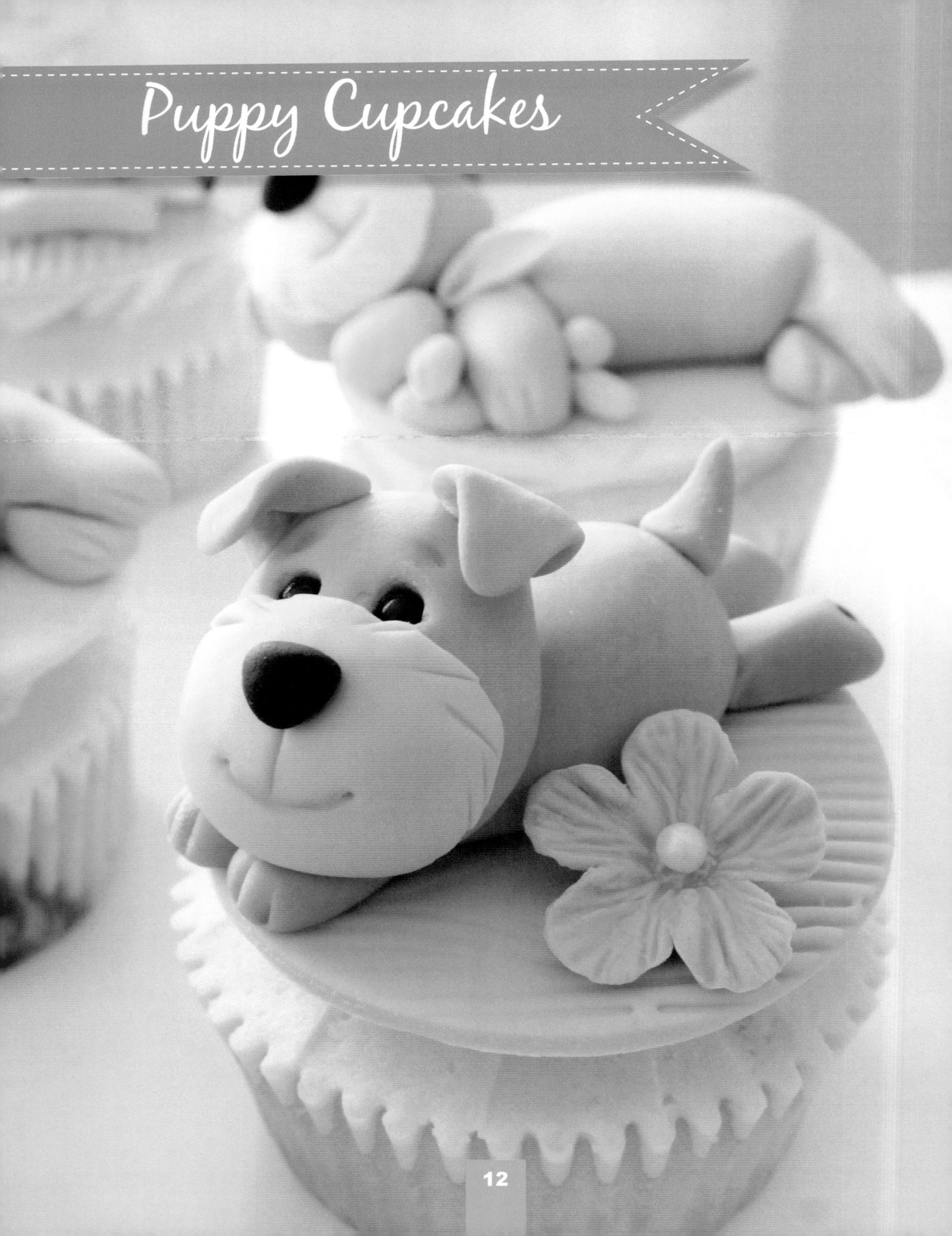

1 Start by rolling a ball of light brown paste then gently shape it into a flat egg shape.

2 For each front paw, roll a long cone shape, then make two cuts on the thicker end for the paw details.

3 Attach these to the body.

4 For the back legs, repeat as above but cut the smaller end to make a flat surface and cut the thicker end on an angle. Then make two cuts to create the paw.

5 Roll a thin, pointy sausage shape for the tail. Attach legs and tail to the body.

6 For the collar, cut a thick blue round shape. Attach this to the neck area and insert a dry spaghetti stick for the head support.

7 To make the head, start by rolling light brown paste into a ball shape.

8 Attach it to the body, sliding onto the spaghetti support.

9 For the nose, thinly roll beige paste and cut it into a round shape.

10 Glue it to the bottom part of the head. Mark some lines for the mouth and fur effect with the veining tool.

11 Roll a small black ball for the nose, and use black sugar pearls for eyes.

12 Attach them to the face.

13 For the ears, roll light brown paste into a cone shape then gently flatten the top and slightly bend the ears.

14 Attach them to the head. Finish it off by dusting the cheek and mouth with pink petal dust and add eyebrows using brown petal dust.

Lazy Dogs

1 I have used a styrofoam sheet, but if you prefer you can also use rice krispie treats for the body of the sofa. Form a main rectangle shape with a higher area across the back.

2 Thinly roll light yellow fondant wide enough to cover the whole sofa. Brush base with edible glue then carefully wrap the fondant around the sofa.

3 Smooth the area and edges with a fondant smoother then use the quilting tool for a stitched effect around the edges.

4 Using the small ball tool, indent 3 dots on the back area. Roll 3 small fondant balls for the buttons and glue them in place.

5 To make the sofa arms/cushions, roll light yellow fondant into a thick sausage and small balls for the buttons.

6 Create a small dot on the centre of one end using the small ball tool.

7 Use the veining tool to mark a star shape to create a tufted look.

8 Glue the buttons onto the finished cushion.

9 Glue the cushions on the sofa at each end.

10 To make the rug, thinly roll mint fondant and cut into a round shape.

11 Using one size smaller round shape cutter, lightly mark it to create a soft line, this will be your guide to making the fringed edging.

12 Make small cuts very close together using a sharp knife.

13 Continue to make this fringing all around the rug.

14 Now they are ready to be arranged on the cake, ready for your puppies!

 **15** To make the puppy, start by rolling white paste into a ball.

 **16** Then flatten it out slightly using the palm of your hand and shape it into a sausage shape.

 **17** To make the paws, roll out more paste into sausage shapes, flatten out the top part then make three cuts.

 **18** Glue them on the body and carefully bend and put the paw on top of each other. Insert spaghetti for a support stick.

 **19** To make the bandana scarf, thinly roll some orange paste, cut into a long triangle shape and make two "comma" shapes.

 **20** Glue this to the neck area.

 **21** To make each back paw, roll a sausage shape, flatten out the top part and make three cuts. For the tail, roll a small "comma" shape.

 **22** Attach the paws and tail on the back side of the body. Make a small diagonal cut on the back of the body to make the leg crease.

 **23** To make the head, roll out more paste and shape it into a ball shape.

 **24** Attach it on the body, over the spaghetti stick.

 **25** For the face, thinly roll out white paste and cut it into a round shape. Next form two small sausage shapes for the eyebrows.

 **26** Attach them to the head and make fur lines and mouth using veining tool.

 **27** Prepare two 4mm black sugar pearls for the eyes and roll a small triangle shaped nose from black paste.

 **28** Attach them to the face with edible glue.

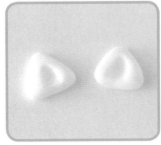 **29** For the ears, roll some paste into a cone shape then gently flatten the top to create a fat triangle shape.

 **30** Attach them to the head. Finish your dog off by dusting the mouth and cheeks with pink petal dust.

1 To make the bones, start by rolling white paste into a sausage shape.

2 Make a small cut on both ends.

3 Thin out the middle area of the bone by rolling it back and forth using your finger

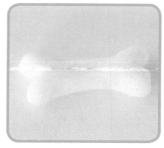

4 Gently open up both of the cut ends, shape and smooth to look like a piece of bone.

5 Roll an oval and flatten slightly. Mark a stitched effect along the face with quilting tool and two dots with a toothpick for eyes. For the nose, roll a small, pink ball.

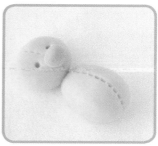

6 For the bunny's body, roll a larger oval shape and flatten slightly. Mark a stitched effect along the body using quilting tool. Attach to the head.

7 For the hands and feet, roll more paste into a long egg shape. Add stitched effect using the quilting tool.

8 Attach them to the body.

9 To make each ear, roll a long egg shape, then flatten slightly. Create the inner ear pleats using the veining tool.

10 Attach them to the bunny.

11 To make the dog bowl, start by rolling orange paste into a ball shape.

12 Using the ball tool, press the centre down and gently rotate it around until you get the right look.

13 Use your fingers to smooth it out and let it dry.

14 Use the black edible marker – you could even write the name of your own puppy!

WOOF!

WOOF!

Materials

Modelling paste:

Light blue

White

Red

Edible pen: black

Edible glue

Tools

Craft knife/scalpel

Paper & pencil

Small paint brush for sugar glue/water

Templates

Square base: 6.5cm x 6.5cm (2 ½" x 2 ½")

Back: as above, with triangle line for the roof

Front: like back, with door cut out

Sides (2): 6.5cm x 6.5cm (2 ½" x 2 ½")

Roof: 7cm x 7cm (2 ¾" x 2 ¾")

1 Cut the paper templates required – one base, one for back, one for the front (with door shape removed), two sides and one for the roof.

2 Thinly roll light blue paste and use the Square Base paper template to trace and cut with a sharp knife. Let this dry completely.

3 For the side walls, do the same as above – cut 2. Scribe some wall lines using a ruler. Allow to dry completely.

4 Cut the back of the house using the template and scribe some horizontal lines as before.

5 For the front house, use the template that has the door shape removed. Mark lines as before and leave to dry completely.

6 Start by gluing one side of the wall to the back of the house. Place an object behind them to hold them together while they bond.

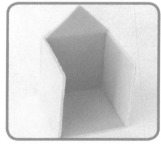

7 Attach the other side wall in the same way.

8 Then attach the front section. Do the same as above and let it completely dry.

9 To make the roof, thinly roll red paste and use the roof template to cut out 2 squares. Cut this square into 3 pieces and leave to dry.

10 Once they are dried, glue them onto the top of the house. Start from the bottom first and finish at the top.

11 Roll out a thick string about 7cm (2 ¾") long.

12 Glue this along the top of the roof.

14 For the name plaque, thinly roll white paste and cut into a slightly curved rectangle. Let this dry. Add a name and glue to front of dog house.

Turtles & Tortoises

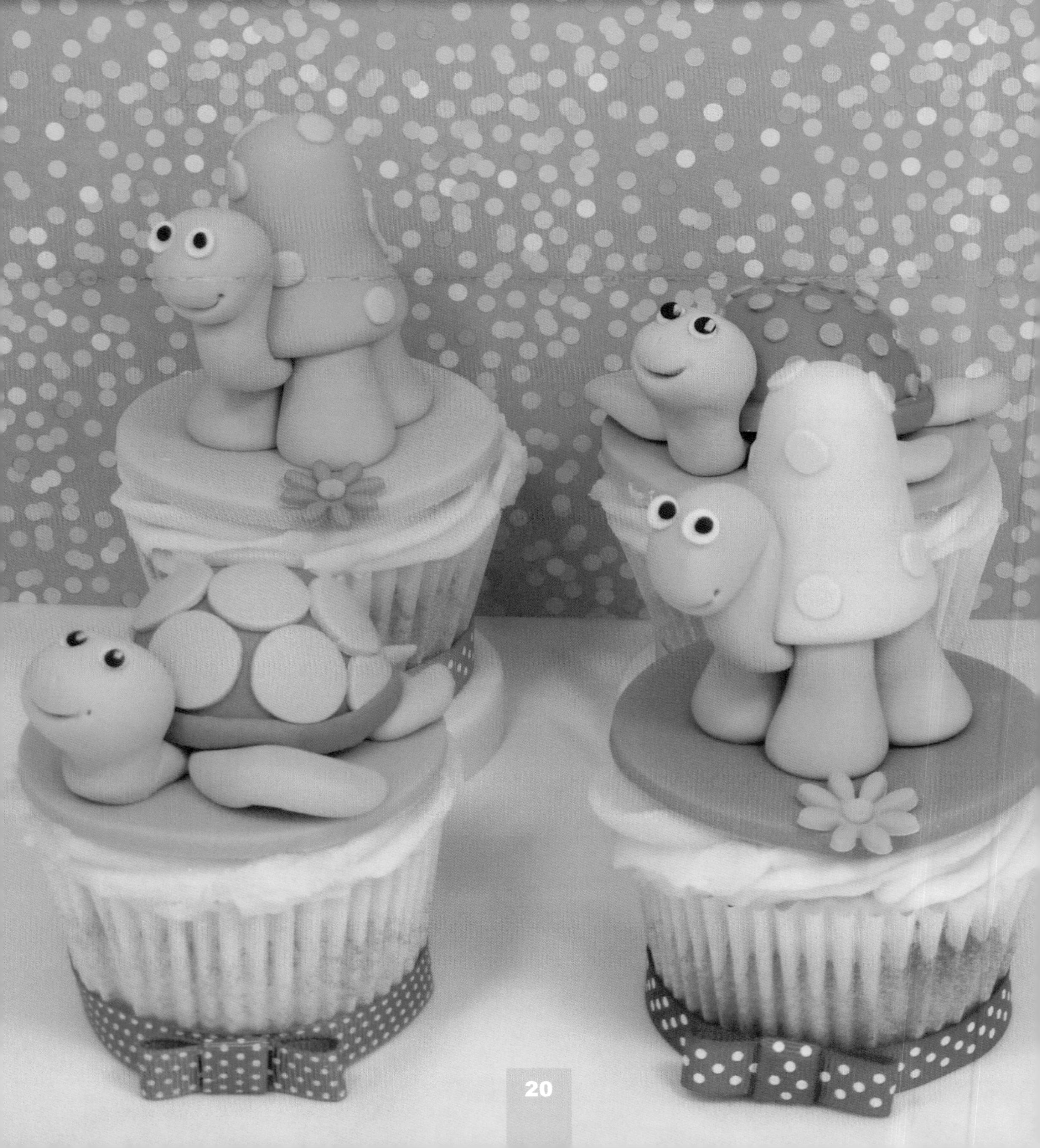

Materials

Modelling paste:

Green
Pink
Yellow
Black
White
Blue
Dark brown
Light brown
Edible glue

Tools

Craft knife/scalpel
Veining tool
Ball tool
Small blossom cutter

1 Tortoise: shape each leg by rolling an oval shape, making it broader at one end. Pinch around the base of the broad end to sharpen.

2 For the shell, shape a cylinder then flatten one end and broaden into a bell shape. Attach to the top of the legs with edible glue.

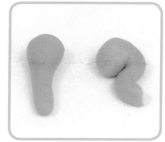

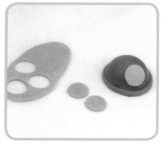

3 Roll contrasting paste for the spots. Use the small round cutter to cut out the spots and glue them to the shell.

4 Shape the head, starting with a short teardrop shape, then push the broad end around to shape the head and neck.

5 Use the larger round cutter to indent a happy smile and indent the ends of the mouth with a toothpick.

6 Take two balls of black and white paste and shape the eyes, gluing to each other then to the head. Glue the neck to the underside of the shell.

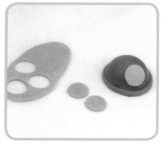

7 Roll out a small amount of paste for the flower. Cut out the blossom using the cutter. Use a contrasting ball of modelling paste in the centre of the flower, securing as before.

8 Shape the turtle shell by rolling a ball then flattening to get a semi circle.

9 Cut a thin strip and wrap around the base of the shell.

10 Roll the lighter brown paste thinly and cut out spots with the medium or small cutter. Glue onto the shell.

11 Shape the front fins from two teardrops, bending to one side to create a fin shape. Glue under the front of the shell.

12 Make the back fins and tail from three teardrops, bending two and leaving the third straight for the tail. Secure in place with edible glue.

13 Shape the head from a cylinder, creating a ball at one end. Mark the eye sockets with the ball tool. Use your knife and cutter to mark the smile and nose.

14 Glue the head in place then add the eyes – adding white then black balls, flattened then glued in place.

Birthday Mice

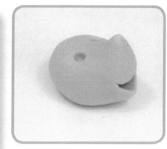

1 For the head, shape a teardrop and draw the point up. Cut the mouth and open it up. Use the ball tool to indent eye sockets.

2 Add a pinch of black then white for the eyes, paint a white dot on the pupils and roll a pinch of pink for the nose.

3 For the ears cut larger round shapes from the grey and smaller from the pink. Glue together, then pinch one side together. Glue to side of head.

4 Roll a pear shaped body and mark the back leg creases with the veining tool. For the feet, shape and mark 2 pink teardrops and glue to body.

5 Shape the arms from grey paste. Roll a sausage, flatten one end, and cut the fingers and thumb using scalpel. Glue to the body.

6 Roll a thin grey sausage for the tail, thinning towards the end. Shape over a piece of kitchen paper until dry then glue to body.

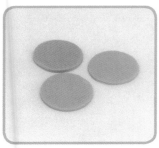

7 For the cake, roll brown paste and cut three medium discs.

8 Roll and cut two pinks discs. Stack and glue them to create the layers of the cake.

9 Shape white paste into a flattened circle, then push parts in and pull parts out to create the splatter effect. Drape over and press to the cake. Secure with edible glue.

10 Roll some small, pink cherries, then a small yellow candle. Add a 'flame' using orange paste. Secure to cake with edible glue.

11 Shape the wedge of cheese in yellow paste and wrap and glue some orange paste around it. Use the scalpel to neaten.

12 Using the small end of the ball tool, indent the cheese to create lots of small dents.

13 Cut round 'cookies' from light brown paste using the small cutter. Indent the cookies with the small end of the ball tool.

14 Roll tiny balls of dark brown paste and glue into the indents of the cookies.

Cheeky Bunny

1 Make a topper disc for each cupcake using brown paste, and set aside to dry. For the bunny's body, roll white paste into a cone shape.

2 For the legs, roll a long sausage shape and cut in half. For the feet, make a flat oval shape, adding paw lines with the veining tool.

3 Glue both legs under the body.

4 Glue the feet onto the legs. Insert a toothpick through the centre of the body and leave to dry.

5 For the carrot, roll orange paste into a cone shape. Add lines with the veining tool. For the green leaves, cut out a daisy shape using a mini daisy cutter.

6 Glue these together and leave to dry.

7 For the hands, roll white paste into a sausage shape, then slightly bend to create a curve. Use the veining tool to make the paw lines.

8 Attach the carrot on the bunny first, then the hands. Let the body dry completely.

9 To make the head, roll a ball shape, then gently shape it into a cone shape.

10 Use your finger to press down to create the nose line. Attach the head to the body.

11 For the eyes, use two 4mm black sugar pearls. Roll pink paste into an oval shape for the nose. Glue all to the face.

12 Use the veining tool for the mouth and a toothpick for the dots on the cheeks. Insert support sticks for the ears. Roll and glue a small ball for the tail to the back.

13 For each ear, roll a sausage shape, then gently shape it into a leaf shape. Use the veining tool to create the ear inner pleats.

14 Carefully insert the ears through the support sticks and glue to the head. Finish off by dusting the cheek, inner ear, mouth and feet with pink petal dust.

Burrowing Bunnies

Materials

Modelling paste:

White

Baby pink

Yellow

Pink

Buttercream, bright green

White sugar sprinkles

Tools

Piping bag

'Grass' piping nozzle (Wilton 233)

Small blossom flower cutter

1 Roll a ball of white paste for the bunny's bottom!

2 Roll 2 small ovals – one for each foot.

3 Roll then flatten 2 smaller baby pink ovals for the base of the foot.

4 Glue the pink pads in place, then use the knife to cut in toe markings.

5 Roll a smaller ball for the tail.

6 Brush the tail with edible glue then roll in sugar sprinkles. Set aside to dry.

7 Use a 'grass' piping nozzle and fill your piping bag with bright green buttercream or frosting.

8 Pipe a 'grass' effect all over each cupcake, pulling 'up' and away each time.

9 Place the bunny body on top of the 'grass' then glue the feet and tail in place.

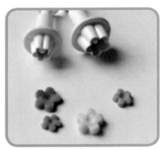

10 Use a blossom cutter to make some small, bright flowers.

11 Roll a small white ball for the centre of each flower.

12 Add to your cupcakes.

13 For a mix of cupcakes you could have grass and small blossoms.

14 Or grass and daisies!

Materials

Modelling paste:
Black
Dark brown
Medium brown
Pink
Teraccota
Green
Peach
Blue
Vegetable shortening: 1g
Petal dust: pink

Tools

Craft knife/scalpel
Veining tool
Extruder & multi-hole disc
Pieces of foam for support

1 Shape a fat sausage of grey paste for the body of the cat. Soften edges, and flatten each end ready for the head and tail.

2 Roll an elongated teardrop for the tail. Cut tip off the thick end and glue to the body. Support with some foam until dry.

3 For each back leg, roll a sausage shape, slightly narrower at one end. Bend at the knee and foot. Indent with veining tool to create a 'paw' effect.

4 Shape the front paws, starting with short sausages, narrowing at the 'wrist' area. Indent the paw section using the veining tool.

5 Add approx.1g of vegetable shortening to pink paste so that it may pass through the extruder to create the 'wool'.

6 Roll a ball of pink and cover in edible glue. Drape the extruded paste over the ball, pressing lightly to secure.

7 Attach strands as before, but at right angles to the first group of strands. Continue to cover the ball until all has been filled in.

8 Glue wool onto the tummy of the cat and glue arms and legs in place.

9 For the head, shape grey paste into a rough triangle, softening the edges.

10 Shape two pinches of grey into triangles for the ears, and glue onto head.

11 Shape the muzzle from an oval of white paste and indent the mouth with the veining tool. Add a small pink nose.

12 Cut jagged white triangles for the whiskers of the cat. Glue to either side of the muzzle.

13 Use pinches of white and black paste to create the eyes, gluing in place.

14 Finish the cat by making hair in the same way as the whiskers, and glue to head, then glue the head to the body of the cat.

15 Black cat: for the front paws roll two teardrop shapes and drape one over the other.

16 Shape more black paste into an oval, place this over the end of the paws to represent the body.

17 Add a pinch of black paste for the tail.

18 For the head, shape an elongated oval. Snip points at each end of the oval, opening slightly, then score to create the effect of fur.

19 Take two pinches of black paste for the ears. Shape into neat triangles and glue to head.

20 An oval of paste will make the muzzle. Indent the mouth section and glue to front of face.

21 Finish the head with two white eyes, add two black pupils and a pink nose. Glue the head to the body.

22 You now have a cute black cat ready to place in his basket!

23 For the ginger cat's body, start with a pear shape, and add a strand of spaghetti through the top to support the head later.

24 Shape two short paws, indenting the front with the flower veining tool. Tuck under the back of the body and glue in place.

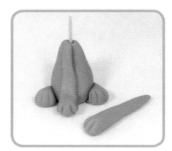

25 For the front paws, shape two elongated sausages, tapering at one end. Indent to create the paw effect as before. Glue in place.

26 Shape the head into a triangle, then soften the points and the edges.

27 Shape the ears from two triangles of paste, with a smaller pinch of paler paste folded inside.

28 Glue the ears to the head, then roll three teardrop shaped pieces of paste and attach between the ears for the hair.

29 Add a white oval for the muzzle, a pink nose and tongue, then small teardrops for the whiskers, textured with a toothpick.

30 Ginger cat is now ready to play!

1 Make a small grey tear drop shape, lifting up the point for the nose of the little mouse toy.

2 Roll a long, thin sausage for the tail and glue in place.

3 Shape two pink teardrops for the ears, flatten them then pinch and gather at one end and glue to sides of head.

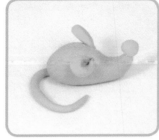

4 Roll a tiny pink nose and glue in place.

5 Roll two small black balls for the eyes and glue in place.

6 Roll a very long, thin sausage then roll it up to resemble a ball of wool.

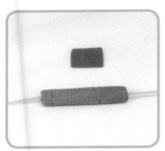

7 Shape a brown paste sausage and insert a toothpick for support. Score to add texture. Cut, dry then glue a blue square on top.

8 Cut a white paste circle and long strip. Glue the strip around the circle to create the bowl.

9 For each fish, roll one large teardrop and two small. Flatten and texture, then glue pieces together.

10 Roll into four little balls and one large ball. Flatten and place together to create the paw prints on the side of cake.

11 For the basket, use a dark brown paste. Roll out and score to add a textured effect.

12 Cut a large circle. And a long, thick strip.

13 Wrap and glue the strip around the edge of the circle to create the basket.

14 For the pillow, shape a square, pinch the corners to soften and fit inside the cat basket.

1 Roll some light green modelling paste into a pear shape for the body.

2 Shape yellow paste into a flat oval. Attach to the chest of the body using edible glue.

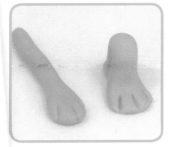

3 Shape each back leg into a long teardrop, flatten and indent at the feet. Bend the legs up and glue to back of body.

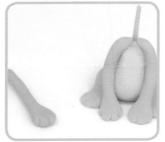

4 Shape the front legs in the same way but don't bend. Glue to front of body. Insert a spaghetti strand into the top to support the head.

5 Roll light green paste into an oval shape for the head.

6 Indent the mouth and smile edges and nose details. Attach the head to the body by inserting onto the spaghetti strand.

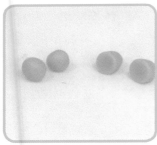

7 Shape the eye sockets by rolling two balls of light green paste and flattening at one end.

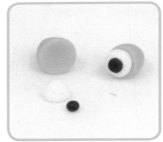

8 Roll then flatten two white balls and two black balls to make up the eyes. Glue them to the eye sockets.

9 Roll a strip of yellow paste approximately 1cm wide. Cut out triangle shapes for crown. Wrap and glue around a small ball of paste.

10 Attach the eyes and crown to the head using edible glue.

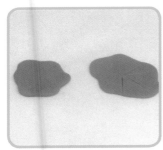

11 Roll out the dark green paste into a rough round shape to create the lily pad. Add texture with the veining tool.

12 Cut out two white blossoms. Add a small yellow ball to one, and curl up the petals towards the centre. Place one on top of the other, glue in place.

13 Make the gift by shaping a rough cube, then work around each edge, pinching and defining the shape.

14 Cut strips of white paste for the ribbon. Shape another strip into a bow and add tails. Glue in place and add some spots if you like!

Hamster & Guinea Pig

Materials

Modelling paste:
White
Pink
Black
Brown
Red
Edible pen: black
Edible glue

Tools

Craft knife/scalpel
Rolling pin
Veining tool
Ball tool
Heart cutter, 4cm (1½")

1 For the guinea pig, mix white and brown modelling paste together, but don't blend too much. Roll into an oval shape.

2 Roll two pinches of brown paste into a teardrop and indent the 'toes'. Tuck under the body and secure with edible glue.

3 For the head, blend white and brown the same as the body, shape into an egg shape and sharpen the end a little more.

4 Indent the mouth then open further with the veining tool. Add a tiny pink tongue and nose. Indent the eye sockets and add two tiny black eyes.

5 Make brown ears as in Step 12. Use the edible pen to add eyelashes and eyebrows.

6 Shape more blended paste into two arms. Roll two teardrops of brown paste for hands. Cut the fingers and thumb with the scalpel.

7 Cut out a red heart, place in front of the guinea pig and glue the bent arms and hands in place, attaching the hearts to the hands.

8 For the hamster, shape an oval of white paste for the body and a ball for the head.

9 Take two pinches of pink modelling paste, shape into elongated teardrop then mark the 'toes' with the pointed end of the flower veining tool.

10 Flatten either side of the head using the veining tool to create the cheeks and nose. Indent to make the mouth and eye sockets.

11 Roll two balls of black paste for eyes, and add a ball of pink paste for the nose. Glue in place.

12 Cut 2 small circles of pink paste for ears. Pinch one side, then push the pinch into the head using the veining tool and glue.

13 Shape the arms from white modelling paste and glue to the body. Roll two teardrops of pink paste for hands then cut in fingers with a scalpel.

14 Cut a pink heart from the remaining pink paste, place in front of the hamster then attach the hands to the heart.

Lazy Lizard

Materials

Modelling paste:

Green

Red

White

Black

Tools

Craft knife/scalpel

Veining tool

Ball tool

1 Shape green paste into an elongated teardrop for the body and tail. Thin it out to a point towards the end.

2 Position the body and tail in place and curl the thin end around. You can support it with foam or kitchen towel until dry.

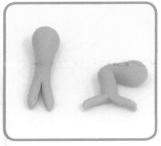

3 To shape 2 back legs and feet: roll a blunt ended teardrop. Cut the thin end in two and bend apart. Bend the leg up.

4 Position and glue next to the body, allowing the two toes to point in opposite directions.

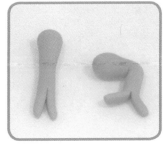

5 Take more green paste for the front legs and make in the same way as the back legs.

6 Glue the front legs in place up against the front part of the body.

7 For the head, create a triangle shape, but with soft edges.

8 Indent the eye sockets with the ball tool, the mouth and nose with the pointed end of the veining tool.

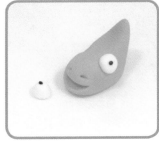

9 Roll two white balls for the eyes, flattening one side slightly. Glue into sockets and add two tiny black pupils.

10 Roll and cut out a long strip of red paste for the tongue. Soften one end and shape into point.

11 Glue the other end of the tongue into the mouth. Curl the pointed end of the tongue up slightly.

12 Take a pinch of black paste and roll into a cigar shape for the body of the fly.

13 Using two tiny pinches of white paste, shape into two teardrop shapes for wings. Glue to the body of the fly.

14 Glue the head onto the body, supporting the tongue with rolled kitchen towel or foam. Glue the fly onto the tongue.

Materials

Modelling paste:
White
Brown
Grey
Baby pink
Beige
Light brown
Black
Edible pen: black
Petal dust: pink
Non-pareils: white
Edible glue

Tools

Craft knife/scalpel
Round cutter, 68mm
(2 ¾")
Leaf shaped cutters, small
Oval shape cutter, small

1 Prepare your modelling paste in the kitten colours of your choice. Combining but not completely blending paste together creates a nice effect.

2 Roll out your paste and cut out each face disc using the round cutter. Leave to dry.

3 Using a leaf shaped cutter, cut two ears for each kitten.

4 Use a smaller leaf shaped cutter to cut two additional pink paste 'inner ear' pieces for each kitten.

5 Attach the pieces together and allow to dry.

6 Roll out a contrasting piece of paste and cut using a small oval cutter. This will form the snout.

7 If the 'snout' looks too large for the face, use the same cutter to trim away the excess length. Do not throw the lefto-ver piece away – we will use this later.

8 Roll a little nose from the paste colour of your choice – pink, black, brown?

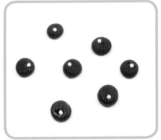

9 Create eyes using small, flat circles of black paste and press a little white non-pareil into each eye to create a pupil.

10 When your head and ear pieces are firm, turn them over and glue on ears.

11 Now add the snout, nose and eyes. Add little eyebrows, if desired, using an edible ink pen.

12 Use your edible ink pen to add the mouth/whisker detail. A little brush of pink petal dust can provide rosy cheeks!

13 You can also can create little fringe details for your kittens using the round cutter.

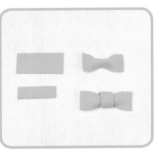

14 For a simple bow, cut two small rectangular shapes (one slightly larger than the other). Pinch the larger piece in the centre and wrap the smaller piece around it.

Crazy Kitten Birthday Party

Materials

Modelling paste:
White, Red,
Baby pink, Grey,
Light brown
Pink
Lilac
Blue
Yellow
Edible paint: white
Edible pen: black
Edible glue

Tools

Craft knife/scalpel
Ball tool
Veining tool
Large piping tip
Fine paintbrush
Scriber/needle tool
Drinking straws
Twine or thread

1 Start by preparing a fondant covered cake in the size of your choice. The number and size of your decorations will be determined by the size of your cake.

2 To create the bunting feature shown, you will need 2 x firm drinking straws. You can cut your straws to size at this stage or wait until you have made the other toppers.

3 Use your scriber/needle tool to pierce a hole directly through the top of each drinking straw.

4 Thread an end of your thread or twine through each straw, creating a 'rope' to hang the bunting. Knot at one end only.

5 Position your bunting posts on your cake, towards the rear.

6 To create the bunting, cut a number of small rectangles of modelling paste. Cut these into diamond shapes, as shown.

7 Drape these shapes over the twine, sticking together with edible glue. Continue until you have enough to fit your cake and knot the twine end in place.

8 For the body of the first cat, create a pear shaped piece of paste.

9 Mark 3 notches in this piece to create the impression of legs.

10 Roll a ball of paste which will form the head of your cat.

11 For facial details, roll two small balls of contrasting paste (whisker area), a small nose and two small triangles to form ears.

12 Glue these on the head of your cat, as shown.

13 Now add eyes and 'whiskers' using an edible ink pen. Edible white paint can be added too to create 'paws' and highlights.

14 To make a party hat, form a cone shape and roll a small ball of contrasting paste.

 **15** Glue these to your cat figure and add more painted details if you wish.

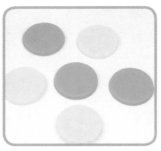 **16** To create the birthday cake, cut a number of contrasting coloured paste circles. Stack together, attaching each layer.

 **17** Cut a single disc of white paste and pull slightly all the way round. This will form your 'frosting' layer. Attach to the top of your cake.

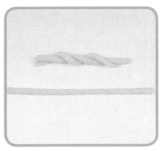 **18** Create cake candles by rolling two contrasting strands of paste and twisting together. Continue to roll until smooth.

 **19** Attach these to your cake and add tiny teardrops of yellow paste to suggest lit candles!

 **20** To create the lying down cat, shape a piece of paste similar to shown – flatter towards the front and bulbous at the back.

 **21** Roll an additional ball of paste to form the head.

 **22** Create forepaws by making the shape shown – flat at back and ball-shaped at the front.

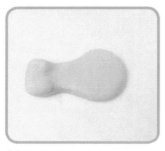 **23** Make the rear legs/paws using the shape shown.

 **24** Attach all legs pieces like this, gluing in place.

 **25** Create a tail by rolling a thin sausage shape of paste and coiling slightly at the end.

 **26** To make the bow, cut a small rectangle of paste and a longer, thinner piece too. Pinch the shorter piece in the middle and wrap the other piece around.

 **27** Attach the head and create all facial features (see Steps 11-13). Attach the bow to the cat and create little notches in the paws.

 **28** You can add little details such as painted dots to the bow, if you wish!

 **29** To create the feeding bowl, roll a small ball of paste.

 **30** Flatten this slightly with the palm of your hand.

31 Create an indentation in the centre with your large ball tool.

32 Use a large piping tip to cut the bowl shape.

33 Use your fingers to smooth the outer edges of the bowl into shape.

34 You can make little fish to fill the bowl by creating small shapes, as shown. Start with an oval shaped piece then pinch in the middle.

35 Trim the 'tail' end with a knife and create little fish features, as desired.

36 To create the cat which grips to the side of your cake, make two forepaw/leg shapes as shown.

37 Roll a ball of paste for the head.

38 Make the body by forming a teardrop shape.

39 Create the facial features as outlined in Steps 11-13 and add to your figure. Attach all pieces to your cake, as shown, using edible glue.

40 Create the rear legs by forming the shapes shown. Start with an oval piece of paste and pinch into shape with your fingers.

41 Glue these leg pieces to your figure and where they touch the cake too

42 The pretty spiral party decorations can be made by cutting colourful strips of paste.

43 Roll these around your drinking straws, as shown, and leave to dry. Remove when firm and trim as required.

44 To make the birthday present, cut a cube of paste.

45 Cut two thin strips of contrasting paste to form the ribbon wrap.

46 Take one strip and place one end over the other. Use the remaining strip to loop over the middle of the first to create a simple bow. Trim as required.

Materials

Modelling paste:
Pink
Green
Light brown
Grey
White
Black
Edible pen: black, brown
Edible glue

Tools

Craft knife/scalpel
Veining tool
Round cutter, 78mm (3")
Foam cupcake dome formers
Extruder gun (optional)

1 Roll out your paste and cut a 78mm (3") circle for each cupcake you're making.

2 Using the sharp end of a veining tool, mark approximately 7 lines across the centre of your paste circle.

3 Turn your circle and mark in the opposite direction, keeping the widths of each 'strand' consistent.

4 Finally, add diagonal lines to the remaining areas.

5 As your paste circle will have stretched a little, use the same circle cutter to trim again.

6 Place your paste circle over your cupcake dome former and allow to dry gently. Once dry add to you cupcakes – some buttercream below will keep the cakes moist.

7 For the kitten's head, roll a ball of paste in the colour of your choice. A tonal effect can be achieved by adding different colours together but not blending completely.

8 For the legs/paws, roll two sausage shaped pieces of paste.

9 Form these into the shapes shown – bulbous at the front (paws) and flatter towards the back (legs).

10 Use your knife to mark 'paws' and glue to your cupcakes dome. Follow this by attaching the head piece on top too.

11 For the ears, cut two triangular shapes. For the snout, shape a small, oval piece of contrasting paste and a small darker nose. Allow to dry.

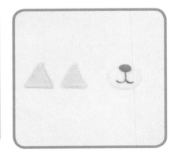

12 Use your edible ink pen to draw a mouth shape, then attach the nose. You can dust the ears with a little touch of pink petal dust too if you wish!

13 Glue on the ears and snout, then and add eyes using your edible ink pen. Using an extruder gun (or roll by hand) create a long strand of 'wool' from softened paste.

14 Drape the strand around your cupcake and attach in the design of your choice.

RECIPES ♥ TUTORIALS

Cake & Bake
ACADEMY
Est. 2014

RESOURCES ♥ INSPIRATION

Oh Baby!
Cute & Easy Cake Toppers for any Baby Shower, Christening, Birthday or Baby Celebration!

Princesses, Fairies and Ballerinas!
Cute & Easy Cake Toppers for any Princess Party or Girly Celebration!

Puppies and Kittens & Pets, Oh My!
Puppies, Kittens, Bunnies, Pets and more!

Tiny Tea Parties!
Mini Food and Tiny Tea Parties That Look Good Enough To Eat!

PLUS:

Passion For Fashion!
Bags, Shoes, Make-up & more!

Pirates & Cowboys!
Ship Ahoy! Yee-ha!

Circus Time!
All The Fun Of The Big Top!

Vroom Vroom!
Trains, Planes, Cars, Diggers & more!

Love, Love, Love!
The loveliest toppers ever!

Over The Rainbow!
A world of rainbow fun!

Xmas Time!
Cute & Easy Xmas Cake Toppers!

and more!

Sugar High Presents...
Cute and Easy CAKE TOPPERS

Brenda Walton and her Sugar High creations are legendary in the cake world. The Cake & Bake Academy bring you Brenda's first ever book! Learn how to make her cute and easy cake topper characters at home.

A MUST for any cake decorator !